CROSS AND CRUCIFIX

RAVENNA CROSS

From a sixth-century mosaic in the apse of the Church
of San Apollinare in Classe, Ravenna. Although the Cross
is depicted, it is the Transfiguration of Christ that is
symbolized. Moses and Elijah appear on either side of
the central disc, while the hand of God appears through
the clouds above. Below the three sheep symbolize the
Apostles Peter, James and John.

CROSS AND CRUCIFIX

*In Christian Worship
and Devotion*

BY

CYRIL E. POCKNEE

LONDON
A. R. MOWBRAY & Co. LIMITED

First published in 1962

PRINTED IN GREAT BRITAIN BY
A. R. MOWBRAY & CO. LIMITED IN THE CITY OF OXFORD
1715

TO MY WIFE

Preface

A CORRESPONDENCE in the columns of the *Church Times* during the months of March and April of last year revealed a widespread interest in the history of the chief symbol of the Christian religion. A letter which I contributed to that correspondence brought me inquiries from overseas as well as from all over England.

While there are a number of monographs in English which deal with certain specialized aspects of the Cross and Crucifix, there appears to be no general survey of the use of the Cross in Christian worship and devotion available. I hope this work may contribute something towards remedying this deficiency.

I am grateful to Professor I. L. Foster, of Jesus College, Oxford, and to the Reverend Richard Tatlock, for reading through the manuscript of this work and for making a number of suggestions and criticisms that have contributed towards a balanced presentation of this important and fascinating subject.

Likewise I am indebted to the Reverend P. J. Dunning, Ph.D., F.R.Hist.S., of St. Mary's College, Strawberry Hill, and Professor Francis Wormold, Litt.D., Director of the Institute of Historical Research, London, for assisting me in tracing the correct source of the Celtic miniature given at Plate 13, which has wrongly been ascribed to the Book of Kells by some of the older ecclesiologists.

I am also indebted to Prebendary G. W. Saunders for information regarding the Lily Crucifix and the influence of the relic of the Crown of Thorns upon the depiction of the Crucifixion in the thirteenth and fourteenth centuries.

CYRIL E. POCKNEE.

TWICKENHAM
Lady Day, 1962

List of Contents

List of Illustrations

ACKNOWLEDGEMENTS

PERMISSION to reproduce the following illustrations is acknowledged:

Plate 31 National Gallery of Art, Washington, D.C.

Plates 11, 18, 22, 23, 24, 26, 27, 28, 29 Victoria and Albert Museum, South Kensington. (Crown Copyright.)

Plate 3 (*b*) British Museum.

Plates 3 (*a*) and 25 Mansell-Alinari.

Plates 7, 8, 9 and 10 Ampliaciones Y Reproducciones Mas, Barcelona.

Plate 32 Canon Donald Rea.

Plate 21 The National Gallery, London.

C. E. P.

PLATE I

A Christian Epitaph

This inscription from the catacombs tells us that the departed person was a Christian who had been signed on the forehead with the chrism in the form of the Chi Rho, and thereby received the gift of the Holy Spirit, here symbolized by the dove. From the catacombs of Callixtus, Rome.

PLATE 2

THE PASSION WITHOUT THE CRUCIFIXION

From a mid-fourth-century carving on the side of a sarcophagus, now in the Museum of Christian Art in the Lateran.

In the centre niche, a wreathed Chi Rho soaring above the Cross symbolizes the resurrection, while on either side, below it, the Roman soldiers are asleep at the tomb. The four side niches are devoted to scenes from the Passion. On the right, Christ is under guard and confronts Pilate, who turns aside from washing his hands, unable to meet the eye of our Lord; on the left the crowning with thorns and Simon of Cyrene complete the theme.

PLATE 3 (*a*)

THE EARLIEST DEPICTIONS OF THE CRUCIFIXION (*a*)

From a carved wooden panel on the door of the Church of Santa Sabina, Rome. Made about A.D. 430. The scene lacks realism.

PLATE 3 (*b*)

THE EARLIEST DEPICTIONS OF THE CRUCIFIXION (*b*)

The first factual portrayal of the Crucifixion, about A.D. 400, upon an ivory casket, now in the British Museum. The artist was concerned for detail. On the left Judas hangs from a tree at the foot of which is a bag with coins.

PLATE 4

THE RABULA CRUCIFIXION

A miniature in the Syriac Gospel written by the monk Rabula in the monastery of St. John in Zagby, Mesopotamia, *circa* 586, and now in the [Medici] Laurentian Library, Florence.

This miniature is of importance as forming the exemplar from which a number of other depictions of the Crucifixion were made. The body of Christ is vested in the colobium. The feet are nailed above the ankles and there is no *suppedaneum*. The head of Christ and that of the B.V. Mary are surrounded by a nimbus. In the background are Mount Gareb and Mount Agra, with which the artist was familiar.

The bearded face of Christ, which appears here, is of oriental origin; and it gradually replaced the iconographic style of the beardless Christ which had appeared in earlier centuries.

PLATE 5

SANTA MARIA ANTIQUA

An eighth-century fresco in the Church of Santa Maria Antiqua, Rome.
It betrays Syro-Greek influence, and has many of the features of the Crucifixion
in the Rabula manuscript (see Plate 4).

PLATE 6

IL VOLTO SANTO

The celebrated Holy Face in Lucca Cathedral, Italy. Made in the eleventh century, it is shown here as it appears on a festival, vested with metal ornaments and a removable crown. It depicts Christ reigning from the tree, the posture of the feet indicates the willingness of the Passion, the figures of the Saints around the girdle and hem of the robe typify the members of the Body of Christ who share in His Cross and triumph.

PLATE 7

A Catalan Majesty

Belonging to the second half of the eleventh century, this carved wooden figure at Baget, Gerona, shows Christ vested as priest and king, reigning triumphant from the Cross.

PLATE 8

A TWELFTH-CENTURY CRUCIFIX

A carved wooden figure from San Juan les Fonts, Gerona, and now in the Diocesan Museum, Gerona. From the first part of the twelfth century, it depicts Christ alive and vested in the colobium.

PLATE 9 and (inset) PLATE 10

Above: A SPANISH MAJESTY—A carved wooden figure decorated in polychrome. Belonging to the early twelfth century, this figure has strong affinities with the Holy Face at Lucca Cathedral, Italy.

Right: CHRISTUS REGNANS—A detail from Plate 9 showing the visage of Christ alive and triumphant. Catalonia is believed to be the source of this type of crucifix, from which the more celebrated Il Volto Santo at Lucca in Italy was derived.

PLATE II

CHRISTUS REX

Limoges enamel on copper-gilt. Made in the thirteenth century, it is part of an altar cross. The figure of Christ, crowned with the diadem and vested in the colobium reaching to the feet, depicts the Crucified triumphing as priest and king over sin and death.

PLATE 12

THE REGENSBURG MINIATURE
(now in the Niedermünster, Munich)
Made for the Abbess Uta (1002–25) this miniature is found on folio 3v of the
Book of the Gospels

Surrounded with signs and sentences which indicate that Christ has
triumphed over death is a tall cross rising through two vesicas to form a figure
of eight. Christ is vested in a robe which reaches only to the knees, and which
differs from the robe of the Catalonian type. The head is crowned with a
circlet against a cruciferous nimbus. The head is inclined, not erect.

PLATE 13

A CELTIC CRUCIFIXION

From a miniature in an Irish Psalter of the second half of the tenth century. The book belonged to the library of St. Martin's Church, Dover, in the later middle ages, and is sometimes called the Southampton Psalter. It is now in the library of St. John's College, Cambridge (MS. 59). Some of the older ecclesiologists mistakenly ascribed this miniature to the Book of Kells in the library of Trinity College, Dublin.

The illustration was undoubtedly made in Ireland as it has all the details associated with Celtic art. Contrary to usual custom, the spear-thrust is in the left side of Christ. The dotted silhouette or outline is believed to be derived from Coptic influence. (See *Proceedings of the Royal Irish Academy*, Vol. LXI (1960), pp. 23–40.)

PLATE 14

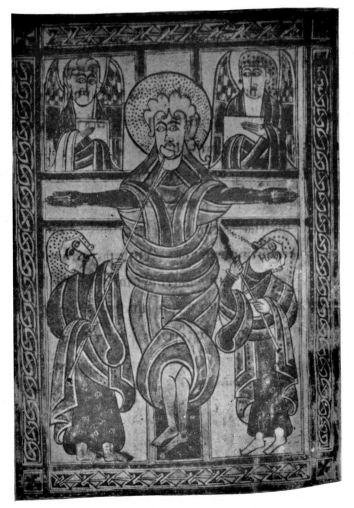

ÉVANGÉLIARE IRLANDIS

From the Book of the Gospels in the library of St. Gall, Switzerland. This illumination was made in the late eighth or early ninth century by a Celtic artist, who was probably one of the monks from Ireland who penetrated down as far as Northern Italy. (See page 46.)

PLATE 15

THE BEGINNINGS OF REALISM

From the Sacramentary of Gellone, made about 780. The head is un-crowned, but the blood is shown flowing from the hands, feet and side.

PLATE 16

THE CROWN OF RUSHES

From a psalter written for a nun of Amesbury Abbey, Wilts., and now at All Souls College, Oxford. Made about 1250, it shows the head with a crown of twined rushes. The feet of the Crucified are crossed over one another and nailed together; whereas the earlier pictures show the feet fastened separately.

32

1

The Sign of the Cross

IF the dating of frescoes in the burial places at Rome and elsewhere, arrived at today by specialists in this branch of archaeology, is correct, then members of the Christian Church were having their tombs decorated with paintings as far back as the first century. These earliest Christian frescoes show no reticence in representing the human form. Some of the pictures relate to stories in the Bible, in which men and women are depicted, as well as animals. Representations of the Deity are usually avoided. God, acting from heaven, is symbolized only by a head or hand.

Amongst the cryptograms found in the Roman catacombs on Christian epitaphs is the monogram of the Chi Rho accompanied by a dove. (See Plate 1.) This is believed to signify the gift of the Holy Spirit given through the anointing in the form of the Chi Rho with the chrism on the brow when the departed person had been initiated into the Christian Church.[1] There seems to be evidence, however, that the Chi Rho was used by the Greeks, and that its use was not unknown in pagan circles.[2]

Events connected with the Passion and Crucifixion are not in evidence. There is no known depiction of the Crucifixion until after the time of Constantine the Great and at the end of the fourth century or the opening of the fifth century. But the use of the sign of the Cross in connection with Christian Initiation was, however, early recognized, since it is found in 'Hippolytus' (c. 215) when the bishop anoints the forehead of the candidate at Confirmation. The same writer also commends the use of the sign of the Cross in private prayer and devotion, 'But imitate him always, by signing thy forehead sincerely: for this is the sign of his Passion.'[3]

As an antidote to the scorpion's sting Tertullian recommends the sign of the Cross, 'We have faith for a defence, if we are not smitten with distrust itself also, in immediately making the sign (of the Cross over the wounded part), and adjuring that part in the name of

---

[1] D.A.C.L., Tome 3, 2211.   [2] *American Journal of Archaeology*, 2 ser. xxxiii, 10.
[3] G. Dix: *The Apostolic Tradition of Hippolytus*, pp. 38 and 68.

C

JESUS.'[1] In private prayer and devotions Prudentius (b. 348) commends the use of the sign of the Cross, in the sixth hymn of his *Cathemerinon*, to remind the Christian of his anointing at Confirmation with the sign of the Cross,

> Cultor Dei memento
> te fontis et lavacri
> rorem subisse sanctum,
> te chrismate innotatum.
>
> fac, cum vocante somno
> castum petis cubile,
> frontem locumque cordis
> crucis figura signet
>
> (Servant of God remember
> the hallowed font's bedewing,
> the signing with the chrism,
> thine inner man renewing.
>
> When kindly slumber calls thee,
> And chastely thou reclinest,
> Upon thy heart and forehead
> See that the Cross thou signest.)

Where we find very early examples of the Cross depicted there is the tendency to disguise it in the form of a cryptogram based on the Greek uncials *Chi Rho* thus: ⳨ or in the form of an anchor.[2] But after 312, when Constantine professed to become a follower of Christ following on the phenomenon which appeared in the sky in the form of a Cross before the Battle of Milvian Bridge, the use of the Cross as a symbol of Christianity in the form of the monogram ☧ becomes more explicit. Eusebius in his *Vita Constantini*, I, 3, written about A.D. 323, describes the standard which Constantine had borne before his armies thus, 'It was a long spear, gilt and provided with a transverse bar like a cross. Above, at the top of this same spear, was fixed a wreath of gold and precious stones. In the centre of the wreath was the sign of the saving Name—that is to say, a monogram setting forth this holy Name by its first two letters combined, the P in the middle of the X. These same letters the emperor was accustomed henceforth to wear on his helmet.'[3]

---

[1] *Scorpiace* (P.L., Tome 2, 122).
[2] Cf. D.A.C.L., Tome 8, 1750–1814; also M. Gough, op. cit., pp. 86–7.
[3] D.A.C.L., Tome 8, 941.

Another factor in the increasing cult of the Cross must have been the discovery of the relic of the true Cross by Helena, mother of Constantine the Great, on Mount Calvary in 326, which she subsequently had set up in a basilica near the spot where the relic was discovered. It was from this discovery that there arose the Good Friday rite of the adoration of the Cross in the church at Jerusalem; and which is described for us by Etheria in the second part of the fourth century.[1]

In the sixth century the relic of the Cross came to be dismembered and broken up into fragments. It was upon the occasion of the reception of one of such fragments at the Monastery of Poitiers on November 19, A.D. 569, that Venantius Fortunatus composed his celebrated hymns in honour of the Cross, *Vexilla regis prodeunt* and *Pange, lingua, gloriosi proelium certaminis*.[2] These hymns, which subsequently passed into the Church's liturgy for use during Passiontide, are different in temper and tone from the Passiontide hymns of the late middle ages, such as *Stabat mater dolorosa*, or those of the baroque period such as *Prome vocem, mens, canoram*. In the hymns of Fortunatus it is the mystery of redemption secured through the triumph of the Cross, rather than the feelings and emotions of the beholder of the sufferings of Christ, which are the theme. Thus:

> beata cuius brachiis
> pretium pependit saeculi,
> statera facta est corporis,
> praedam tulitque tartari.

> (Blest tree, whose happy branches bore
> The wealth that did the world restore;
> The beam that did the body weigh
> Which raised up hell's expected prey.)

> Pange, lingua, gloriosi
> proelium certaminis,
> et super crucis tropaeo
> dic triumphum nobilem,
> qualiter redemptor orbis
> immolatus vicerit.

[1] M. L. McClure and C. L. Feltoe: *The Pilgrimage of Etheria*, pp. 74–6; also L. Duchesne: *Christian Worship*, pp. 510–11.   [2] F. J. E. Raby: *Christian-Latin Poetry*, pp. 88–91.

(Sing, my tongue, the glorious battle,
Sing the ending of the fray,
O'er the Cross, the victor's trophy,
Sound the loud triumphal lay,
Tell how Christ, the world's redeemer,
As a victim won the day.)

In Syria in the second century it seems to have been the custom to indicate the east, towards which the worshippers turned in prayer, by inscribing a cross on the wall.[1] While prayer towards the east may have pagan and pre-Christian origins, since it was connected with the worship of the rising sun, it also developed a significance connected with the Second Advent and the Parousia, as it was believed that the return of Christ would be heralded in the east by the sign of the Cross in the heavens.[2] This belief was based on the words of Christ, 'Then will appear the sign of the Son of Man in heaven' (*St. Matt.* xxiv. 30).[3] Likewise, to pray towards the east in private as well as liturgical devotions was accompanied by the setting up of a cross of wood. Thus in the apocryphal *Story of John, the Son of Zebedee*, we read, '(John) took a cross of wood and put it up towards the east and kneeled and was praying.'[4] In the same story the conversion of a multitude of people by the apostle, John, is followed by prayer towards the east, '(the people) turned their backs to the west and fell down on their faces before the cross to the east, and were weeping and saying: We worship thee, Son of God, who wast suspended on the tree. And the procurator was lying prostrate before the cross.'[5]

The use of a wooden cross seems to have been known in North Africa about A.D. 200 as Tertullian writes, that while pagans worship images carved from wood, Christians prefer a plain wooden cross thus, 'As for him who affirms that we are "the priesthood of a cross," we shall claim him as our co-religionist. A cross is, in its material, a sign of wood; amongst yourselves also the object of worship is a wooden figure. Only, whilst with you the figure is a human one, with us the wood is its own figure.'[6] In the next chapter of the same treatise he continues, 'Others, with greater regard for good manners, it must be confessed, suppose that the sun is the god of the Christians, because it is a well-known fact that we pray towards the east, or because we make Sunday a day of festivity.'[7]

[1] E. Peterson: *La Croce e La Preghiera verso oriente* in *Ephemerides Liturgicae*, LIX, pp. 52–3, Rome, 1945.   [2] F. J. Doelger: *Sol Salutis*, Münster, 1925, p. 217.   [3] Peterson: op. cit., p. 64.   [4] W. Wright: *Apocryphal Acts of the Apostles*, vol. 2, p. 5, 1871.   [5] Ibid., p. 32.   [6] *Ad Nationes*, c. 12.   [7] *Ad Nationes*, c. 13.

In Syria the plan of some of the early churches was such that the celebrant and worshippers faced east during the liturgy; and the assumption frequently made that the celebrant in the pre-Nicene period always faced the people behind the altar cannot be sustained in the case of these churches[1] since the altar in the third century was placed close to the eastern apse; and there is reason to believe that a cross was engraved in the middle of the apse,[2] so that the celebrant and people praying towards the east saw the emblem of the Second Advent, the sign of the Son of Man. The writer of the *Didascalia*, written about A.D. 230, says, 'Let the lay men sit in another part of the house towards the east. For so it should be, that in the eastern part of the house, the presbyters sit with the bishops, and next the lay men, and then the women also. For it is required that you pray toward the east, as knowing that which is written: *Give ye glory to God, who rideth upon the heaven of heavens towards the east.*'[3] The author is quoting verse 33 of Psalm lxviii according to the Septuagint text.

The rites connected with the dedication of a church were gradually developed in imitation of those connected with Christian Initiation. Thus, in the eighth century, we find both the altar and the walls of a new church received a lustration of holy water at the hands of the bishop. Likewise, in imitation of the sealing with chrism after baptism, both altar and walls were anointed with chrism in the sign of the Cross.

The anointing of the walls does not appear in evidence until the eighth century; and it becomes a feature of the Gallicanized Roman ritual introduced into France in the reigns of Pepin (*d.* 768) and Charlemagne (*d.* 814). At first the bishop simply signed the interior walls of the new church in a number of places with the chrism,[4] and until the thirteenth century this appears to have been the usual custom.[5] But after that time the number of anointings came to be specified as twelve within the church,[6] and in later instances another twelve signs were made on the exterior walls.[7]

Also in the late middle ages the places that were to receive the anointings with chrism were previously painted in red, and sometimes carved in stone or modelled in plaster. The commonest form of such crosses was the cross *patee*.[8]

[1] D.A.C.L., Tome 15, 1880–84. See also, M. Gough, *The Early Christians*, pp. 60, 134–6.
[2] Peterson: op. cit., pp. 65–6.   [3] R. H. Connolly: *Didascalia Apostolorum* (1929), pp. 119–20.
[4] M. Andrieu: *Les Ordines Romani*, Tome 4, p. 345 (Louvain 1956).
[5] R. W. Muncey: *A History of the Consecration of Churches*, p. 68 (1930).
[6] H. A. Wilson: *The Pontifical of Magdalen College*, p. 115 (1910).
[7] W. Maskell: *Monumenta Ritualia Ecclesiae Anglicanae*, Vol. 1, 220–1 (2nd ed., 1882).
[8] Muncey: op. cit., p. 67.

2

The Advent of the Crucifix

WE have already remarked upon the absence of the Crucifixion of Christ from the early frescoes in the Roman catacombs. This cannot be unconnected with the apostolic and early patristic emphasis on the Resurrection of Christ. St. Peter's sermon on the day of Pentecost clearly points to the glorified and triumphant Lord as the centre of Christian devotion, 'This Jesus God raised up, and of that we are all witnesses. Being therefore exalted at the right hand of God, and having received from the Father the promise of the Holy Spirit, He has poured out this which ye see and hear' (*Acts* ii. 32–33). The references in St. Ignatius of Antioch (*c.* A.D. 110) and St. Justin Martyr (*c.* A.D. 160) to Sunday as the day of the Lord's resurrection clearly indicate the emphasis on the triumph of Christ over sin and death. Hence any depiction of Christ crucified would have been regarded as a kind of anachronism. There was no reluctance to portray the human figure in Christian art in the second and third centuries as we can see in the Roman frescoes; but the complete absence of any depiction of the events connected with our Lord's Passion and of the Crucifixion itself cannot be accidental; and it accords with the emphasis on the resurrection and glorification of Christ.

It is not until the mid-fourth century that we find on a marble sarcophagus, now in the Lateran Museum, Rome (see Plate 2), scenes from the Passion of Christ. There are five panels in relief on one side, two present Christ before Pilate, another Christ bearing His Cross, and the last a soldier crowning Him, the crown being a crown of glory rather than a crown of thorns. The central panel should, according to later and modern notions, show the Crucifixion, but the reticence and theology of the period did not permit this. Hence this central panel contains a plain cross with doves seated on its arms, and it is surmounted by the Chi Rho emblem, wreathed in the crown of immortality. On the ground are two soldiers, one waking, one asleep.[1]

The fact, however, that this sarcophagus depicts scenes from Christ's Passion indicates a change that was gradually to appear in

[1] R. Garruci: *Storia dell' arte cristiana*, Tome 5, Plates 349–51.

Christian teaching and devotion. Some few years after this carving was made we find the two earliest Christian depictions of the Crucifixion that are known to us. One of these is on a panel of an ivory casket, now in the British Museum. (See Plate 3 (b).) The other is on one of the doors of the Church of Santa Sabina, Rome. (See Plate 3 (a).) The first of these examples is dated about A.D. 400, and is the first factual portrayal of the Crucifixion in all its stark realism.[1] The other, which is carved in wood, is dated about A.D. 430.[2]

It is appropriate, at this point, to consider the question of the extent to which the representations on crucifixes of the details of our Lord's death are accurate and literal. Two items are in question: the foot-support, and the clothing.

It is clear from secular writers that a wooden block (termed *sedile* or *cornu*) was fixed in the middle of the upright beam so as to stand between the victim's legs and carry the weight of the body. Such a fixture would not be seen, but because of its presence the legs could be free, nailed, or bound according to the wish of the executioner, and without any further support. It is to be noted that in the earliest portrayal of the Crucifixion (*c*. 400, Plate 3 (b)) no foot-support is suggested, and it may reasonably be conjectured that this is due to the fact that the details of crucifixion (which was abolished by Constantine, *d*. 337, but employed sporadically for some time later) were still sufficiently well and commonly known for the absence of a foot-support to cause no puzzlement. Later on, when the details of crucifixion had been forgotten and realism in portrayals of the crucifixion came to the fore, it was logically but ignorantly assumed that a foot-support was necessary, and it was consequently shown in sculpture and painting.

Concerning the next-earliest portrayal of the Crucifixion (*c*. 430, Plate 3 (a)), Gough[3] rightly points out that the scene lacks realism, and conjectures that the artist could have had no first-hand knowledge of crucifixion. This conjecture is open to question. Ignorance is not the only possible explanation of artificiality; lack of knowledge cannot be held to explain the disproportionate size of the figures. In any case, there is again no suggestion of the two feet nailed to a foot-support, as appears in later representations.

Our Lord is variously represented as wearing either a meagre loin-cloth or a 'skirt,' or as fully-clothed. The last form of dress, from the evidence of Scripture, is clearly symbolic and not at all

---

[1] M. Gough: *The Early Christians* (1961), p. 180.   [2] Ibid., p. 180.   [3] Op. cit., p. 180.

factual. Was our Lord, therefore, clothed in any way at all? Once again, the earliest portrayals represent him as clothed with a meagre loin-cloth. This accords with the evidence of secular writers as a possibility, but it was equally common for the victim to be crucified naked. A balance of evidence in favour of our Lord wearing a loin-cloth, such as is seen in Plates 3 (*a*) and 3 (*b*)—but not conclusive evidence—is provided in the Talmud. Rabbi Judah (*b*. A.D. 135) says that: 'About four yards from the stoning-place they stripped off the criminal's clothes, covering a male in front, but a female both before and behind.'[1]

Although our Lord's death was contrived in the Roman fashion by crucifixion and not in the Jewish fashion by stoning, it seems reasonable to suppose that the Romans would be compelled by public opinion to respect Jewish convictions concerning the dignity of a human body, howbeit a 'criminal's,' and that the representations in Plates 3 (*a*) and (*b*), are not only early, but factual. The later 'skirt' is not as factually accurate.

Earlier than these two Christian portrayals is the blasphemy in the form of a *graffito* or scribble on the wall of a house on the Palatine in Rome. It depicts an ass crucified, with a man standing close by, his arms raised in prayer. Below a contemptuous legend reads: 'Alexamenos worships God.' It has been suggested that Alexamenos was a slave, now become the butt of his fellow slaves for his belief in Christ.[2]

Nevertheless, the desire to depict the Crucifixion in the early fifth century was still exceptional, and it was to be several centuries before it found a ready acceptance in the West. St. Gregory of Tours tells us in his work *De gloria martyrum* (Chapter 22), written about 593, that a painting of the Crucifixion had to be veiled because of the opposition it aroused in those who saw it in the church at Narbonne.

The absence of any depiction of the Passion and Crucifixion from the fifth- and sixth-century mosaics at Ravenna fully accords with the older ideas. At Ravenna the symbol of the Cross is in evidence in more than one instance, both in the orthodox and Arian churches; but such crosses are always the *crux gemmata*, made of gold and decorated with jewels, or sometimes with floriated terminals, and accompanied by the Greek uncials *A* and *Ω* . In the Church of San Vitale, Archbishop Maximinianus of Ravenna holds a short jewelled

---

[1] *Sanhedrin*, fol. 42, 49, 52. Cited p. 206 in *A Talmudic Miscellany*, by P. I. Hershon, Trübner, 1880.
[2] Gough, op. cit., pp. 83-4.

cross, but there is no figure on it. In San Apollinare in Classe, the basin of the apse has the cross of triumph surrounded by stars. It is the same in regard to the mosaics at Rome. In the Church of San Stephano Rotondo, built in the middle of the seventh century, the basin of the apse shows the *crux gemmata* surmounted by a medallion of the bust of Christ, over which appears the symbol of the hand of God.[1] In the Church of SS. Cosmo E Damiano, the *Agnus Dei* with the book of the seven seals is displayed with the cross behind it. About this time crosses with the *Agnus Dei* in the central motif or medallion begin to appear. A celebrated cross of this type is the *crux vaticana* at St. Peter's, Rome, given by the Emperor Justin II (565–78) to Pope Gregory the Great.[2]

It is to the East, however, that we must look for the theological impetus in depicting the Crucifixion. This arose out of the Christological controversies, notably the Monothelite heresy, which tended to emphasize the divinity of Christ to the exclusion of His humanity. This, in turn, led to the idea that the sufferings of Christ were unreal since the divine will completely obliterated His human will. The sixth oecumenical Council held at Constantinople in 681, condemned this heresy and also decreed, 'That instead of the Lamb, our Lord Jesus Christ shall be shown hereafter in His human form in the images; so that without forgetting the height from which the Divine Word stooped to us, we shall be led to remember His mortal life, His Passion, and His Death, which paid the ransom for mankind.'[3]

The Monothelite heresy was, however, a more subtle form of the earlier Monophysite heresy, which agitated Eastern Christendom in the fifth and sixth centuries. In Syria Monophysitism was particularly entrenched and it provoked an orthodox reply in the form of the Rabula Gospels, written in 586,[4] in which the Crucifixion is depicted with an element of realism which underlines Christ's sufferings through His human nature. This miniature (see Plate 4) is of importance since it was to provide an exemplar which was to persist in East and West for many centuries. Nevertheless, although there is an element of realism in the Rabula Crucifixion, it is not realistic in a manner that the crucifix became in the later middle ages and the baroque period.[5] Christ is vested in a long purple tunic known as the *colobium* which emphasizes His priesthood and kingship; and it will be noticed that there is no crown of thorns on his Head, which is

---

[1] See D.A.C.L., Tome 3, 3081–2. [2] See D.A.C.L., Tome 3, 3113–21.
[3] J. Hefele, *Histoire des Conciles*, Tome III, 573; also Mansi, Tome XI, 978–9.
[4] D.A.C.L., Tome 3, 3074–5. [5] L. Bréhier: *Les Origines du Crucifix*, pp. 34–5.

outlined against the nimbus or halo. The sun and moon which appear on the left and right of the cross introduce an element of dramatic realism into the picture, since they are intended to convey the darkness which came over the earth from the sixth to the ninth hour (*St. Matt.* xxvii. 45). These symbols were subsequently to appear in many later pictures of the Crucifixion.

Two other examples, based on the Rabula miniature, may be cited. In the catacomb of St. Valentin there is a seventh-century fresco, part of which has been mutilated. It is the first example of the Crucifixion in the Roman catacombs, and its date should be noted.[1] The other example is the fresco in the Church of Santa Maria Antiqua, Rome. (See Plate 5.) Both examples show Christ vested in the colobium down to the feet, His arms are stretched out straight, and His eyes are open, as in the Rabula miniature. It is not until the tenth century that Christ is depicted with His eyes closed on the Cross.[2] In these three examples the legs, and not the feet, are nailed separately to the Cross above the ankles; and the feet are unsupported by the footstool or *suppedaneum*.

Other examples of crucifixes belonging to this period include the pectoral cross given by St. Gregory the Great to Queen Theolinda of the Lombards. This cross is now in the Treasury at Monza. The figure of Christ is clad in the colobium reaching to the feet, and the head is uncrowned but outlined against the nimbus.

By the opening of the eighth century this type of crucifixion was to be found on religious monuments and ornaments, both in East and West. Painters, sculptors, goldsmiths, miniaturists and embroiderers all contributed to this work. One consequence of the iconoclastic controversy in the East was the emigration of monks to Italy who upheld the veneration of images and crosses. It should not be forgotten that there was a considerable colony of Greeks and Syrians in the city of Rome who were sufficiently influential during the seventh and eighth centuries to appoint Popes who were either Greek or Syrian by race. The presence of these orientals at that time explains the eastern character of the depiction of the Crucifixion in Rome, of which the fresco in Santa Maria Antiqua is a well-known example. In all of them, almost without exception, the style of the Rabula Crucifixion has been copied with some modifications. It is to be found not only on frescoes, but also on portable and pectoral crosses.[3]

---

[1] D.A.C.L., Tome 3, 3084–7. [2] W. de Grüneisen, *Saint Marie Antique*, p. 336, Rome, 1911.
[3] D.A.C.L., Tome 3, 3087–9.

This type of crucifix depicts Christ in a long robe reaching to the feet, but without sleeves. The head has no crown of thorns, but is usually outlined against a halo or nimbus. It has been asserted by more than one authority that Christ crowned with a diadem and vested as a priest-king derives from Eastern Christendom, but no evidence has been found to support such a view.

Something must be said in regard to the celebrated Holy Face of Lucca, *Il Volto Santo*. (See Plate 6.) Stripped of its modern ornaments, including the crown, the figure is vested in a long-sleeved tunic which almost touches the feet. The legend that this crucifix was carved by Nicodemus and that it was miraculously conveyed to Italy in the eighth century is not now seriously entertained.[1] There is no reference to *Il Volto Santo* before 1070, and the workmanship is of eleventh-century design. It is likely that this crucifix is of Catalan origin, and there are a number of extant examples known to us still in Spain.[2]

The influence of the Lucca Rood was, however, considerable, and examples copied from it are to be seen in places as far apart as the Cathedral of Brunswick in Germany, and at Langford, Oxon, England. It is possible that guilds of merchants from Lucca, which vied with Venice and Florence in foreign trade, may have taken this idea of the crucifix with them. Arnolfini, whose picture with that of his wife, hangs in the National Gallery, London, was a member of the Lucca Guild in Bruges. There also seems to have been a copy of the Lucca Rood at the Abbey of Bury St. Edmunds in the middle ages as the *Liber Albus* (Harl. 1005) records, 'The altar of St. Peter in the front of the Church at the feet of St. Edmund (i.e. at the East end) was dedicated when Baldwin was prior, but it is not known by whom. But the Holy Cross which was set up in that place is very holy and ancient. Some say it was there before the monks' time; others that Abbot Leofstan (1044–65), when he went to Rome, had it made according to the measure of the Cross at Lucca.'[4]

We have already suggested, however, that the type of crucifix which is sometimes called 'Christus-Rex' has its origins in Spain, and particularly in Catalonia. One such example, to be seen in the Museo de la Ciudalela, Barcelona, belongs to the late eleventh century.[5]

[1] E. Mâle: op. cit., p. 254, also R. Garruci: op. cit., Tome 1, p. 594.
[2] A. K. Porter, *Spanish Romanesque Sculpture*, Vol. 1, pp. 8–12.   [3] E. Mâle: op. cit., p. 256.
[4] M. R. James: *Abbey of St. Edmund at Bury*, p. 139 (1895).
[5] A. K. Porter: op. cit., Vol. 1, Plate 34.

An early twelfth-century example is to be seen at San Juan Las Fonts, Gerona,[1] and another at Baget, Gerona. There is a further example at Las Caldas de Montbúy, Barcelona of the early twelfth century. These are all full-sized crucifixes of carved wood. (See Plates 7, 8, 9 and 10.) The tunic has long sleeves, some of the heads have a diadem, others have not. From Spain this style appears to have spread over the Pyrenees into France, as we can see in the examples still at Belpuig[2] and La Lagonne, in the Spanish and French Pyrenees. Examples farther north are the Saint Sauveur Roods at Amiens,[3] Rheims and Chartres. These all have the arms straight out and the sleeves reach to the wrists, as in the Catalan examples cited. Altar crosses with Christ crowned and vested as priest and king in Limoges' enamel are found in the thirteenth century (see Plate 11), but a twelfth-century example of an altar cross in this style is to be seen in the Episcopal Museum of Vich, Catalonia.

It has sometimes been supposed that this type of crucifix originated in Germany, since a miniature exists in the Regensburg Gospels, made for the Abbess Uta (1002–25). But an examination of this miniature (see Plate 12) shows that it differs considerably from the Catalonian type. The robe only reaches just below the knees and the head is on one side and not erect in the true Christus-Rex style. Further, the head is crowned with a circlet and not a true diadem. In any case it must be emphasized that the Regensburg miniature was not intended as an object of veneration or devotion in the same manner as the full-scale Catalonian and French examples to which we have made reference.

The British Isles contain numerous examples of Celtic art and culture, including monumental and churchyard crosses. Some of these are incised, and others are sculptured in the round. In many instances the entire cross is subordinated to ornament and decoration. The head of the Celtic cross is most frequently in the form of a ring or wheel.[4] It is not unlikely that this design is adapted from the Chi Rho monogram, which was frequently encircled by a ring.

The earliest forms of the cross, however, known in the British Isles are simple incisions on stones belonging to the fifth, sixth and seventh centuries. In Wales distribution of such monuments is predominantly westerly and coastal, notably at Anglesey in the north and Pembrokeshire in the south. The inscriptions on such monuments

---

[1] Porter: op. cit., Vol. 2, Plate 65.   [2] E. Mâle: *L'Art Religieux du XIIe siècle*, p. 255.
[3] L. Bréhier: *L'Art Chrétien* (1928), p. 260.   [4] D.A.C.L., Tome 2, 2939–47.

show they are either of Celto-Irish or Latin origin.[1] The Chi Rho emblem is found with some of those bearing Latin inscriptions.

But cross-decorated stones are more frequent in those of a later date, between the seventh and ninth centuries. The widespread diffusion of these cross-bearing monuments is to be correlated with the adoption of the cross as a Christian symbol in the fifth century A.D.[2]

Besides the cross-forms certain of the monuments are exceptional in bearing crudely drawn figure representations. Two of these are of special interest as representing early renderings of the Crucifixion. These are thought to belong to the seventh century. In both instances Christ is shown clad in a long tunic coming down below the knee, with arms outstretched, and eyes open. One of these is at St. Dogmaels, Cardiganshire, and the other is at Llanychaer.[3] The representations of the Crucifixion on these monuments are comparable to those met with on Byzantine and Coptic depictions of the sixth and seventh centuries.[4]

At Llanbachraith, Anglesey, is the upper portion of a sculptured wheel-head cross. The front is filled with the figure of Christ (incomplete), shown as a beardless youth, apparently undraped, facing front, with arms outstretched just below the level of the shoulders with palms outwards. The rendering is similar to the Crucifixion-representations met with in Ireland on the so-called 'Crosses of the Scriptures,' belonging to the tenth century.[5]

From the ninth to the eleventh century we find sculptured crosses and cross slabs which represent the culminating development of Welsh early Christian art. A number of these are characterized by the use of the cross, either in the round as a free-standing monument, or in relief as a shaped cross-slab. Viking influence is discernible in some of these crosses, such as that at Penmon, Anglesey.[6]

The vigorous native talent and skill that informed and sustained Irish structure through the stresses of the Viking period and produced some of its greatest masterpieces in the tenth and eleventh centuries, were lacking in Wales; and the dying flickers of Welsh Christian art were finally extinguished by the Norman Conquest.[7]

Depictions of the Crucifixion on stone crosses in Ireland in the earlier period show Christ robed down to the feet with his eyes open

[1] V. E. Nash-Williams: *The Early Christian Monuments of Wales* (1950), pp. 7–13.
[2] Nash-Williams: op. cit., pp. 17–27.   [3] Ibid., p. 104 and Plates XVII–XVIII.
[4] Ibid., p. 191.   [5] Ibid., p. 53 and Plate LXIX.   [6] Ibid., p. 65 and Plate XXI.
[7] Ibid., p. 31; see also D.A.C.L., Tome 2, 2942–50.

and with his arms out straight. The earliest of these is at Cardonagh, County Donegal, belonging to the end of the seventh century.[1] This is an outlined and incised depiction of Christ surrounded by four persons; and it has affinities with the style of the Crucifixion depicted on the Rabula manuscript. (See Plate 4.)

Not until the twelfth century, when Celtic influence was on the wain in Ireland, does Christ appear without the long robe on the cross, and enveloped only from the waist downwards, as at Glendalough, County Wicklow.[2]

Of equal interest to the monumental Celtic crosses are the depictions of the Crucifixion to be found in illuminated manuscripts by Celtic artists. The human figure is often grotesquely delineated and the colour appears crude and unnatural; but the result is a wonderful brilliance of colour and intricacy of geometrical designs. The features of the human figure are made to fit with the scheme of interlacing and spirals.

Within the scheme the Crucifixion figures are fully draped and the eyes of Christ are open. On each of the arms of the Cross there is either an angel or a bird. The superscription is usually absent. The two soldiers, Longinus and Stephaton, are generally present on either side of the Cross, one holding the spear, and the other the sponge on the reed. (See Plates 13 and 14.) Probably the earliest of these Celtic miniatures is that in the Durham Chapter library,[3] dated *circa* 670, in which the details described above are all in evidence. The Book of Kells, which is the best known of all Irish Gospel-Books, has, however, no depiction of the Crucifixion. But there is one in the *Évangéliare Irlandis*, in the monastic library of St. Gall, Switzerland, written in the late eighth or early ninth century. We now know that during the seventh and eighth centuries Celtic monks penetrated down through France and Switzerland into Northern Italy, as we can see from the St. Gall manuscript, the *Lectionary of Luxeuil*, and from the Turin Gospels and the Bobbio Missal.[4] The most notable of these Celtic missionaries was St. Columbanus, who died at Bobbio in 615.

---

[1] F. Henry, *La Sculpture irlandaise*, Vol. I, p. 161 (Paris 1933).　　　[2] Ibid., pp. 129–130.
[3] J. E. Hunt: *English and Welsh Crucifixes*, p. 8.　　　[4] D.A.C.L., Tome 2, 939–61.

3
Towards Realism

THE Carolingian era, which we should date from about A.D. 750, witnessed a change of emphasis in Christian teaching and devotion which affected many aspects of Christian worship. The causes of such changes were partly psychological, and are to be found in the Teutonic temperament which is more inclined to introspection and morbidity than the Latin mind. The conversion of the Franco-German peoples to Christianity under Charlemagne (*d.* 814) is reflected in an increasing emphasis on the Passion of Christ and of realism in regard to the details of the Crucifixion.

Already we can see it in an incipient form in the comment of the Venerable Bede (*d.* 735) on the antiphon sung on Sundays at the asperges (a ceremony introduced into the Mass in the eighth century), *Vidi aquam egredientem de templo a latere dextro* ('I saw water flowing from the right side of the temple'). According to Bede the door of Solomon's temple was on the right, so it was the right side of the Saviour, which was to be opened by the thrust of the lance.[1] This tradition of the lance penetrating the *right* side of Christ's body was to persist throughout the middle ages. Medieval commentators were to insist that the priest detaches at Mass, at the moment of the fraction, a small part of the right side of the Host to symbolize the wound made by Longinus in the right side of Christ.

It is with the Carolingian crucifixes that we first encounter the blood gushing from the wound in Christ's side, as we can see in the Crucifixion depicted in the Sacramentary of Gellone, belonging to the late eighth century. (Plate 15.) Later medieval teaching was to develop this idea and to teach that this wound was the door of grace through which the devout soul could penetrate to the heart of Jesus. It was from this devotion to the wound in Christ's right side that ultimately the devotion to the Sacred Heart of Jesus was to come into existence. This we can see adumbrated in the Dominican liturgy of the thirteenth century which had a feast of the Wound in the side on the day which later came to be fixed for the Feast of the Sacred Heart.[2]

[1] Bede: *In libros regum* (P.L., Tome 91, 722) and *De templo Salomonis* (P.L., Tome 91, 753-4).
[2] L. Gougaud: *Devotional and Ascetic Practices in the Middle Ages* (1927), pp. 95-6.

Another contributory cause to the depiction of the Crucifixion in a realistic manner was the mysterious reception by St. Francis of Assisi on a certain day in September, 1224, at Mount Alvernia, of the marks of the stigmata on his hands and feet, and a fifth bleeding wound was opened in his side. From then onwards interest in the five wounds of Christ became a dominant interest and theme in medieval devotion.

In 1239 King Louis IX of France received in Paris the reputed Crown of Thorns from Constantinople. This relic was housed in La Sainte Chapelle, which the King had built as a shrine; and on the occasion of the consecration of this superb edifice the hymn *Si vis vere gloriari* was composed.[1] The cultus of this relic gave an impetus to the depiction of Christ wearing the crown of thorns, which until then was not usually the custom on crucifixes and pictures of the Crucifixion. The reputed Crown of Thorns is now kept in the Cathedral of Notre Dame de Paris; and an examination of it shows that, in fact, it is a wreath of rushes rather than intertwined stems with thorns on them. This fact may explain why the earliest form of the crown of 'thorns' shown in the thirteenth-century manuscripts (see Plate 16) is in the form of a wreath of rushes and only later does a thorn-like crown appear in pictures of the Crucifixion.

It is necessary to say something in regard to the crowning of the head of Christ in the depiction of the Crucifixion. As we have already remarked the earliest pictures and crucifixes show the head outlined against a halo or nimbus; but the head itself is not crowned in any way. In the New Minster Psalter (see Plate 17), executed about 1099, we see the first kind of crown which consists of a fillet or circlet of gold. A similar kind of fillet seems to have been worn by Anglo-Saxon bishops as a mark of honour.[2]

It has sometimes been supposed that Saxon crucifixes were always with an uncrowned figure; but the evidence in the New Minster Psalter does not support this view. Also contemporary and important evidence is to be had from William of Malmesbury (*c.* 1095–1143) in a chapter entitled *De alia cruce de qua cecidit diadema* in his work on the *Antiquities of the Church of Glastonbury*. 'There is another very ancient cross there also, which used to stand in the refectory. On a certain day King Edgar and Archbishop Dunstan were sitting at meat in the refectory . . . when, wonderful to relate, the wooden image

---

[1] For an English version of this hymn, see *English Hymnal*, No. 97.
[2] See Pocknee: *Liturgical Vesture* (1960), p. 43.

PLATE 17

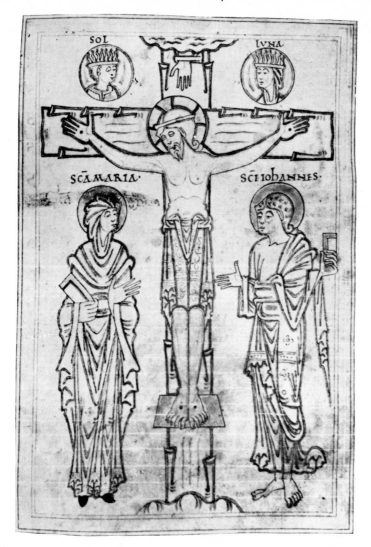

THE FILLET OF HONOUR

From the New Minster Psalter made at Winchester about 1099. The head of Christ is surmounted by a band or fillet of gold. This seems to be the earliest form of the crown, and it preceded the crown of thorns by some centuries.

PLATE 18

A DANISH CRUCIFIX

Made about the middle of the twelfth century in latten, this figure is typical of the style found throughout the Scandinavian countries in the last part of the middle ages in which the head is usually surmounted by a diadem.

PLATE 19

A NORWEGIAN ROOD SCREEN

This interesting example forms part of the early twelfth-century wooden or 'Stave' Church at Urnes. It will be noted that the figures of the B.V. Mary and of St. John are crowned as well as that of the Crucified.

PLATE 20

THE LILY CRUCIFIX

A fifteenth-century carving on the central mullion of the East window of the South aisle in the Parish Church of Wellington, Somerset.

The lily plant has budded into five flowers symbolizing the five wounds of Christ. The late medieval idea that Good Friday was 25 March meant the association of the Passion and the Annunciation of our Lady.

PLATE 21

A Renaissance Crucifixion

Painted by Raphael, 1483–1520, and now in the National Gallery, London.

Two angels hold phials to contain the blood from the wounds in the hands and side of Christ. Following the later tradition the feet are nailed one over the other.

There is a note of serenity which is heightened by the Tuscan landscape which forms the background.

PLATE 22

ALTAR AND PROCESSIONAL CROSS

Made at Limoges. Copper-gilt with champlevé enamel set with pastes and an amethyst. Thirteenth century. The hand of God appears at the top of the cross, symbolizing the presence of God the Father, accepting the sacrifice of the Son.

This type of cross could be stood on a socket at the back of the altar after it had been detached from the processional staff.

PLATE 23

SPANISH PROCESSIONAL CROSS

Made at Tarragona in the middle of the fourteenth century. Silver-gilt, enriched with translucent enamels. Central motif of the Resurrection of Christ.

PLATE 24

AN ITALIAN ALTAR CROSS

Florentine workmanship, about 1460. Silver-gilt with translucent enamels.
Central motif, St. Francis of Assisi surrounded by angels, prophets and saints
of his order: St. Clare, St. Louis of Toulouse, St. Bonventure and St. Anthony
of Padua.

PLATE 25

A FIFTEENTH-CENTURY PROCESSION

A fresco painted by Pinturicchio in 1498 showing the enthronement procession at St. John Lateran of Pope Pius II. The painter has conveyed with detailed accuracy the ceremonies of the occasion.

The processional cross has arms of equal dimensions, and is without any corpus or figure. The altar cross is of small proportions, and is also without a corpus. The absence of candlesticks on the altar will also be noted.

PLATE 26

A VOTIVE CROSS

Made in the ninth century, of Carolingian-Lombardic origin. Cloisonné enamels with cabochon pastes on gilt copper. The ring under the cross was intended for votive offerings to be suspended over or near the altar.

PLATE 27

A CROSS RAGULY

A Spanish processional cross about the middle of the sixteenth century. Copper-gilt with silver, parcel gilt figure.

PLATE 28

COVER FOR A BOOK OF THE GOSPELS

French, thirteenth century, Champlevé enamel on copper-gilt. The symbol of the hand of God appears from a cloud over the top of the cross (see also Plate 22). Christ crowned as a victor puts down death, symbolized by the skull under His feet.

PLATE 29

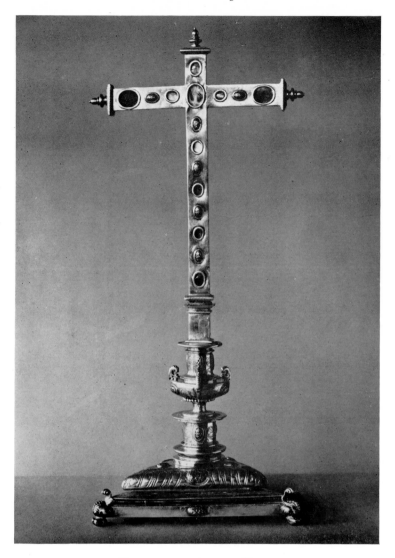

RELIQUARY ALTAR CROSS

Made in Spain about 1630. Silver-gilt with enamel bosses which enclose relics of the saints. The absence of a figure at this late date should be noted.

PLATE 30

THE RELIC OF THE CROWN OF THORNS

In 1238 Baldwin II, the Latin Emperor of Constantinople, pledged this reputed relic as security for a loan. King Louis IX of France undertook to pay off the loan in exchange for the relic, which was received in Paris in August 1239. La Sainte Chapelle was built as a shrine to house it.

It will be observed that the crown is without spines, and is, in fact, a crown of plaited rushes. For the influence of this crown upon the late medieval design of the crowned head of Christ see page 48.

PLATE 31

THE APOTHEOSIS OF REALISM

Painted by Matthias Grünewald (Mathis Nithardt-Gothardt, 1460–1528), it represents the Crucifixion with both anguish and realism. There is a real crown of thorns on the head, and the eyes are closed in death. The body of Christ is lacerated with the marks of scourging.

This picture, known as the 'Small Crucifixion', is to be distinguished from a similar one by the same artist on the Isenheim triptych at Colmar, Germany.

PLATE 32

ANCIENT AND MODERN

A modern rood and its loft restored by the late Sir Ninian Comper over the medieval screen at Eye, Suffolk.

of the Lord affixed to the cross shook itself from head to foot, so that the jolt caused his diadem to fall between the King and the Archbishop.'[1]

Also there is the well-known crucifix of Saxon origin on the wall of the cloister garth at Romsey Abbey, Hampshire. No crown now remains, but it is almost certain that there was one originally there as the head is very flat and on it at the top is a hole, doubtless for fixing the crown.[2]

In Scandinavia the head of the Crucified was frequently crowned with a diadem, both in the case of the smaller metal crucifixes belonging to the twelfth and thirteenth centuries (see Plate 18), and also in the case of the crucifix which was displayed on the rood beam not only was the head of Christ crowned with a diadem, but also the attendant figures of our Lady and St. John were treated likewise. The interesting example of the Norwegian Stave Church at Urnes (see Plate 19) belongs to the early twelfth century, and has a rood of this kind.[3]

We have already remarked upon the impetus given to depicting the head of Christ crowned with thorns by the acquisition of the reputed Crown of Thorns in 1239. Even so, only gradually did this type of crown come to be accepted as the norm in carvings and pictures of the Crucifixion. Examples still exist from the thirteenth century of the crown being simply a band with a spiral tie. (See Plate 16.) After 1239 we find examples of the crown as follows:

(1) A band or fillet of rushes bound with a spiral tie;
(2) The spiral tie is tightened, so that the rushes tend to bulge outwards;
(3) The tie is thickened and the fillet becomes a twisted cable of two cords or strands;
(4) The points of the cable are represented as thorns;
(5) The fully developed Crown of Thorns.

It was believed in the middle ages that the Crucifixion took place on March 25, and thus Good Friday and the Annunciation of the Blessed Virgin Mary came to be associated with one another.[4] This is reflected in the post-Communion Collect for Lady Day (now used

[1] P.L., Tome 179, 1698.
[2] For a detailed discussion of Saxon crucifixes, see T. A. Kendrick: *Anglo-Saxon Art to A.D. 900* (1938); also W. G. Collingwood: *Northumbrian Crosses of the pre-Norman age* (1927).
[3] Anders Bugge: *Norske Stavkirken*, (Oslo, 1953), pp. 13–14, 18; also J. Strzygowski: *Early Church Art in Northern Europe* (1928), pp. 118–22.
[4] E. Mâle: *L'Art religieux en France du XIIIe siècle* (Paris 1913), p. 244.

E

as the Collect of the Day in the Book of Common Prayer), which says, 'that as we have known the Incarnation of thy Son Jesus Christ by the message of an angel, so by His Cross and Passion we may be brought to the glory of His Resurrection.'

From this idea there seems to have developed in the late thirteenth or early fourteenth century a peculiar form of the crucifix of which a number of examples on carved wooden screens and misericords, stained glass windows, on stone carvings on tombs and the mullions of windows, still exist. This type of crucifix is perhaps best described as the 'Lily' crucifix.[1] The development of the idea may be summarized as follows:

(1) In the thirteenth century the Annunciation is symbolized as taking place in the spring-time by the placing of a pot of flowers in scenes depicting that event;
(2) In the fourteenth century, the flowers become lilies;
(3) The Crucifix is placed on them to associate March 25 as Lady Day and the day of the Crucifixion;
(4) The figure of Christ hangs on the lily plant, which in some instances has budded into five blossoms, symbolizing the five wounds.

While the Lily Crucifix is known to us from one or two continental examples, e.g. an alabaster carving at Cologne, the most numerous examples are in England, such as the stained glass window in the chapel of the Queen's College, Oxford, belonging to the early sixteenth century, the tomb of John de Tannersley (d. 1414) in St. Mary's Church, Nottingham, the tomb of William Earnley (d. 1545) in West Wittering Church, Sussex. Other examples will be found at Tong, Shropshire, York Minster, Long Melford, Suffolk, Wells Cathedral, and Wellington, Somerset. (See Plate 20.)

Only gradually, and after many centuries, did the Crucifixion of Christ come to be portrayed or depicted in a realistic manner; and only at the end of the middle ages did this realism tend to excessiveness. This idea was continued by Renaissance painters such as El Greco in Spain and Matthias Grünewald (who should more probably be known as Mathis Nithardt-Gothardt, 1460–1528) in Germany. (See Plate 20.) But in Italy Raphael (d. 1520) introduces a note of serenity into his celebrated painting of the Crucifixion. (See Plate 21.)

---

[1] See W. L. Hildburgh in *Archaeologia*, Vol. LXXIV (1925).

4

The Rood and Its Crucifix

As early as the fourth century it was customary to separate the altar from the choir and nave by a low marble wall with an opening in the centre. This low wall supported a number of porphyry columns, which in turn supported a beam or architrave. Thus the whole structure formed an altar screen. This we know was the case with old St. Peter's, Rome,[1] built in the time of Constantine the Great, and also in the case of other Roman basilicas. But this type of screen is to be distinguished from the Rood Screen which formed such a feature of English parish churches and cathedrals as well as monastic churches in the second part of the middle ages. The altar screen of the Roman basilica stood immediately outside the sanctuary, whereas the Rood or Choir Screen enclosed the choir as well as the altar.

It does not seem to have been the custom to surmount the altar screen of the Roman basilica with a large crucifix and attendant figures of our Lady and St. John. Further consideration, therefore, of this type of screen falls outside the scope of this work.

With the possible exception of Spain, the Choir or Rood Screen at the entrance to the chancel was a development in Northern Europe; and examples are to be found in Scandinavia, the British Isles, France, the Low Countries and Germany. It does not seem possible to state exactly when this type of screen first came into use. But in England the first evidence is after the Norman Conquest,[2] and this would accord with the piety and development of certain aspects of religious beliefs of the late middle ages.

In earlier times there were frequently two ambons or pulpits, one on either side of the choir, from which the Epistle and Gospel were chanted at the Eucharist. In the second part of the middle ages the two separate pulpits disappeared with the enclosure of the choir in monastic and conventual churches. Over the Choir Screen, which now formed the enclosure, there ran a continuous gallery or loft from which the liturgical lections were read, notably on Sundays and

[1] See D. Fontana: *Templum Vaticanum* (Romae, 1694), pp. 89 and 91; also E. Pistolesi : *Il Vaticano Descritto*, 8 vols. (Roma, 1829–38).
[2] For a somewhat earlier date, see: F. E. Howard and F. H. Crossley, *English Church Woodwork*, pp. 216–18.

festivals. The enclosure of the choir became necessary with the vast increase in pilgrims to the shrine of the Saint whose body had previously lain under the altar, but which under the new cultus was now placed in a separate shrine behind the high altar, as is still the case of St. Edward the Confessor at Westminster. The pilgrims were thus able to pass up the north and south choir aisles without disturbing the offices being recited by the Community in choir. A similar arrangement once prevailed at St. Albans Abbey, Christchurch Priory and Winchester Cathedral.

In cathedral and monastic churches the Choir Screen was frequently termed the pulpitum. Over the screen and its loft there was usually a beam with a large crucifix and the figures of our Lady and St. John, and sometimes attendant angels. The scheme was quickly copied by parish churches, and medieval examples still exist in most Northern European countries. (See Plate 19.) Thus the worshipper entering a parish church in the later middle ages saw the Rood beam with the scene of Calvary at first sight rather than the altar which was hidden by the Choir Screen below.

Not infrequently the chancel arch, against which the Rood was set, was boarded in to form a tympanum which had the 'doom' or last judgement painted on the side facing the nave. Thus the Cross of Christ appeared silhouetted between the worshipper and the final judgement, thereby illustrating the medieval prayer, 'Set thy Cross and thy Passion between thy judgement and our souls, now and at the hour of our death.'

The figures on the Rood beam were usually shrouded with a great veil during Lent, which was only let down during the singing of the anthem 'Hail our Monarch'[1] at the end of the procession on Palm Sunday.

After the Reformation in England Choir Screens were frequently erected until the eighteenth century, but the crucifix disappeared and its place was sometimes taken by the royal coat-of-arms. A notable Jacobean screen is to be seen at Tilney All Saints, Norfolk.

Since the Catholic Revival of the last century screens have been erected with the Rood above; and in some instances where a medieval screen has remained *in situ* a modern Rood beam with its crucifix has been erected over it. (See Plate 32.)

---

[1] See *English Hymnal*, Appendix, p. 902.

5

Pectoral and Reliquary Crosses

THE custom of wearing a cross on the breast suspended by a cord or chain round the neck appears to have been known since the fourth century; and examples of this type of cross or emblem exist from periods which antedate any written or documentary reference to the custom.

In 1863 a tomb in the ground outside the Church of San Lorenzo fuori le Mura, Rome, was found to contain such a cross made of gold with a small cavity containing a relic of the reputed true Cross.[1] Crosses of this kind were frequently worn, not merely by ecclesiastics, but by devout lay persons also. In many instances such a cross was, in effect, a portable reliquary, since it contained a cavity for a relic of a saint or a relic of the wood of the true Cross. But there were also simple crosses of devotion worn on the breast which were not reliquaries, but were made of metal without any kind of artistic decoration or any cavity for relics. Such have been found at Carthage in excavations belonging to the fifth and sixth centuries.[2]

When the coffin of St. Cuthbert (d. 687) was opened in 1827 at Durham it was found to contain a pectoral cross of seventh-century craftsmanship belonging to that saint.[3] The central cavity, which was covered by a precious stone, probably contained a relic. (See Plate 33.)

It should be underlined that pectoral crosses of this kind were in the nature of articles of personal devotion and they were in no sense ensigns of ecclesiastical office or status.

It is now customary for many Anglican bishops to wear a pectoral cross as an insignia of episcopal rank. This is an innovation that has only come into use since the opening years of the present century. The first Archbishop of Canterbury to wear a pectoral cross was Dr. Randall Davidson (d. 1930), as the portraits of successive Archbishops in Lambeth Palace clearly testify.

As an ensign of episcopal rank in the West, the pectoral cross was unknown until after the Reformation. It is, in fact, a Counter-

---

[1] De Rossi: *Bull. di archeol. crist*, 1863, p. 31; see also D.A.C.L., Tome 3, fig. 3051.
[2] D.A.C.L., Tome 3, 3105–6.   [3] C. F. Battiscombe: *The Relics of St. Cuthbert* (1956), pp. 308–24.

Reformation ornament, and first mentioned (p. 162) in the *Caerimoniale Episcoporum*, published at Rome in 1606, under Pope Clement VIII. The learned Roman Catholic, Dr. Daniel Rock, remarks: 'What we may say of England may be with the same truth said of the whole Church; and it is remarkable, that while both Pope Innocent III and St. Thomas of Aquino are most minute in reckoning up the vestments and ornaments distinctively belonging to bishops in their days, and always worn by them when solemnly arrayed for the holy sacrifice, those two writers never drop a word about the pectoral cross.'[1]

It is when we come to consider the *encolpion* worn by bishops in the East to-day that we get confirmation of the idea that the pectoral cross was in origin a portable reliquary. In the East the encolpion did not become an ensign of episcopal rank until the middle ages. By that time it had become simply an oval medallion with a picture of Christ or the Blessed Virgin Mary on it.[2] But St. John Chrysostom (*d.* 407) in his nineteenth homily on the Statues mentions the original custom of the encolpion being worn by many Christian people as a portable reliquary.

The modern Roman ritual also testifies to the original custom since a bishop is ordered to say: *hanc Crucem sanctorum tuorum reliquiis refertam*,[3] when he assumes the pectoral cross. It is perhaps necessary to point out that the terms 'pectoral' and 'encolpion' both mean 'on the breast,' and that the custom of certain Anglican prelates wearing such a cross on the abdomen has no kind of sanction or authority.

Relics, both of the wood of the reputed true Cross, as well as the relics of saints, were also incorporated into processional crosses; and at a later date when it became the custom to have a standing cross on the altar as a permanent feature, relics were sometimes incorporated into the arms and centre of the cross. (See Plate 29.)

---

[1] D. Rock: *The Church of our Fathers*, Vol. II, p. 143.
[2] S. Salaville: *Introduction to the study of Eastern Liturgies* (1938), p. 175.
[3] *Missale Romanum. . . . Leonis XIII auctoritate recognitum Romae*, Desclée, 1911, p. lii.

6

Processional and Altar Crosses

WE have already alluded to the ensign which Constantine the Great had carried before his soldiers after the official recognition of Christianity in the Roman Empire. Eusebius leaves no doubt in his description that this was in the form of a cross (see p. 34).

The first reference to the use of a cross in a religious procession, however, is that given by the lawyer Socrates (*d. circa* 439) in his *Church History*, in which he tells of the attempt by St. John Chrysostom, at the end of the fourth century, to combat the nocturnal processions of the hymn-singing Arians by instituting similar processions for orthodox believers, and he continues, 'There were invented by John silver crosses for them on which lighted wax tapers were carried at great expense by the Empress Eudoxia.'[1] Evidence in the late fifth century points to the use of processional crosses at Tours on which were mounted candles in a similar manner.[2] At Rome a fresco in the catacomb of Pontianus, belonging to the seventh or eighth century, shows a cross with jewels surmounted by candles.

The Venerable Bede (*d.* 735) tells us in his *Ecclesiastical History* that Augustine and his fellow monks in 597 carried for a banner a silver cross and the image of our Lord and Saviour painted on a board as they went to meet King Ethelbert for the first time after landing on the shores of Kent; and as they walked they sang litanies. So also a little later they came to Canterbury with the holy cross and the image of Christ upraised.[4]

Ordo XXI compiled about the year 750 describes the litany procession on April 25 at Rome. The procession is led by the poor of the *xenodochio*, before whom is carried a painted wooden cross. After these come the seven stational crosses, having on them each three lighted candles. Then follow the bishops, priests and subdeacons, and finally the pontiff and his deacons, before whom are borne two crosses.[5] There are numerous references in the ninth

---

[1] P.G., Tome 67, 689.   [2] M. Andrieu: *Les Ordines Romani*, Tome III, p. 241.   [3] Ibid., p. 241.
[4] P.L., Tome 95, 56 (*At illi Augustinus et socii veniebant, crucem pro vexillo ferentes argenteam et imaginem Domini Salvatoris in tabula depictam laetaniasque canentes . . . fertur autem quia appropinquantes civitati, more suo cum cruce sancta, et imagine magni Regis Domini nostri Jesu Christi, hanc laetaniam consona voce modularentur*). See also, C. Plummer: *Opera Historica*, Tome I, pp. 45-6 (2nd ed. 1946).
[5] Andrieu, Tome III, p. 248.

century to the jewelled cross carried before the Pope, including the one which was presented by Charlemagne.[1] When Pope John I (523–25) visited Constantinople he was met by the people of the city carrying crosses.[2]

Ordo XX, compiled in the middle of the eighth century, describes the procession on the feast of the Purification of the Blessed Virgin Mary. Seven crosses were carried, which the Latin text describes thus, *Interim egrediuntur cruces VII, portantur a stauroforo permixti cum populo*.[3] The use of the Greek term *staurophores* to describe the cross-bearers is an indication of contemporary Byzantine influence in Rome, as also is the use of crosses bearing lights. Such crosses with lights (λαμπάδων) were used in Constantinople at the beginning of the fifth century.[4]

Mabillon's Ordo XI, *auctore Benedicto*, compiled about 1140, describes the candlemas procession in the twelfth century at Rome. From this we learn that the regional subdeacon took the stational cross from the altar and it was kissed by all before being carried in procession before the pontiff.[5] It is probable that the stational cross originally stood by the side of the altar; but by the twelfth century it had become the custom to remove it from its shaft and place it in the middle of the altar on a socket. When the stational processions fell into disuse in the later middle ages the cross became in some instances a permanent feature of the altar. But there are plenty of examples of altars without a standing cross in the late middle ages; while in other instances the custom of having a combined processional-cum-altar cross was continued. (See Plate 22.) The inventory of the Church of St. Dunstan-in-the-East compiled in 1550 shows that this custom had persisted into the sixteenth century, 'In primis a greate Crosse of Sylver and gylt with bervall in the myddes with a Crucyfyx Mary and John weing j^e xvj ounces; It'm a ffote of Copper and gylt for the greate Crosse weyinge (blank).'[6]

Many processional and altar crosses of the late medieval and renaissance periods have no figure of the Crucified upon them (see Plates 23 and 24); and in the Roman rite the altar cross with the figure of Christ upon it only became *de rigueur* after 1746.[7] Prior to that date books of Roman ceremonial, such as the *Caeremoniale Episcoporum*,

[1] M. Andrieu: *Les Ordines*, Tome III, p. 242.   [2] L. Duchesne: *Liber Pontificalis*, Tome 1, p. 275.
[3] M. Andrieu: *Les Ordines Romani*, Tome III, p. 236.   [4] Ibid., p. 241.
[5] J. Mabillon: *Museum Italicum* (Paris, 1687), Tome 2 (*Subdiaconus vero regionarius elevat crucem stationalem de altari, quam plene portat in brachio, ut osculetur ab omnibus, in processione ante pontificem, usque in exitu ecclesiae; deinde levat eam erectam*).   [6] H. B. Walters: *London Churches at the Reformation* (1939), p. 243.
[7] *Constit., Accepimus Benedict XIV* (July 16, 1746).

PLATE 33

THE PECTORAL CROSS OF ST. CUTHBERT

This cross was discovered with St. Cuthbert's body when his coffin was opened in 1827. There can be little doubt that it belonged to him, and was worn during his lifetime. It was in no sense an ensign of episcopal office, but rather was an emblem of personal devotion.

It is of seventh-century Anglo-Saxon workmanship, made of gold with cloisonné sections, and a central boss made from a garnet, which covered the cavity containing a relic. The cross as seen here is after its cleaning and repair by the experts at the British Museum. It is now kept in the Chapter library of Durham Cathedral with the other relics of St. Cuthbert.

PLATE 34

THE ANGLICAN TRADITION

This engraving shows the choir and sanctuary of St. Paul's Cathedral about the year 1700. The altar is furnished with a pair of candlesticks of medium proportions. There are also two wine flagons and a large paten or 'tazza' for the Eucharistic breads. In accordance with post-Reformation Anglican practice before the Oxford Movement there is no standing cross.

Rome, 1606, display woodcuts of the altar cross without any figure. (See also Plate 25.)

In England the altar cross was first stipulated by Richard, Bishop of Chichester in 1246. It is mentioned in the same century by Durandus (d. 1296). In the twelfth century Pope Innocent III writing before 1198, when he became Pope, in his *De Mysterio Altaris*, says, 'On the corners of the altar two candlesticks are set which, with the cross in between, bear lighted tapers.'[1] Before that century there appears to be no conclusive evidence for the use of an altar cross in the West. The older custom required that nothing should stand on the altar save what was needed for the celebration of the Eucharist, and this would have precluded both cross and candlesticks. No doubt the growing emphasis on the Passion of Christ in the last part of the middle ages contributed towards the desire to have a cross or crucifix on the altar. In some instances there was a reredos which incorporated a crucifix in the central panel. In medieval England the reredos in parish churches was usually long and low, and the crucifix contained in the central panel would have been a small one intended to stimulate the devotion of the celebrant. There is, however, evidence that votive crosses were sometimes suspended before altars as early as the eighth and ninth centuries.[2] Such crosses were of comparatively small proportions; and sometimes they were suspended from the corona or candelabra that hung before altars, and sometimes they were hung independently. (See Plate 26.)

There was also in some instances a small cross surmounting the ciborium which stood with its four columns over the altar in the earlier centuries.[3] But such a cross was of relatively small proportions in comparison with the canopy of which it formed the apex.

In the thirteenth century in England it was the processional cross which was regarded as essential as the constitutions of Winchelsey, Peckham and Archbishop Gray of York all show.[4]

In Lent a wooden cross was carried in processions without any figure on it,[5] and this was usually painted red.[6] On Palm Sunday two crosses were used at Salisbury and elsewhere: the Lenten cross leading the main procession, while a silver one was carried before the second procession with the relics.[7]

[1] P.L., Tome 217, 811.   [2] D.A.C.L., Tome 3, 3103–4.   [3] E. Bishop, *Liturgica Historica*, p. 22.
[4] W. Maskell, *Monumenta Ritualia Ecclesiae Anglicanae* (1882), Vol. 1, p. cxxii.
[5] W. H. Frere, *The Use of Sarum* (1898), Vol. 1, p. 219.
[6] C. Wordsworth: *The Tracts of Clement Maydeston* (1894), p. 49.
[7] W. G. Henderson: *Processionale Sarum* (1882), pp. 47–51.

We have already noted that towards the end of the middle ages the more usual place for the display of the large crucifix was at the entrance to the chancel on the Rood beam in parish churches, and over the pulpitum in monastic and collegiate churches.

It has been suggested by some earlier commentators, including Baronius, that we have much older evidence for the use of a cross standing on the altar in the third Canon of the Council of Tours, A.D. 567.[1] But this is not the case, since the Canon in question refers to the arranging of the Eucharistic particles in the shape of a cross on the altar, after the fraction, a custom observed in the Gallican and Mozarabic liturgies[2] as well as those of Eastern Christendom. Vast and towering altar crucifixes are chiefly a product of the later baroque period and the Counter Reformation, and they are also in evidence in Lutheran churches.

In the Church of England since the Reformation the use of an altar cross has from time to time been the subject of controversy and complaint. In the Chapel Royal there was a cross or crucifix on the altar during the reign of Queen Elizabeth I, to which the Puritans and more extreme reformers objected. It is difficult to ascertain from the inexact language used whether this cross had a figure on it.[3] Similar complaints were made about Archbishop Laud in the middle of the seventeenth century.[4] Nevertheless it would be true to state that the majority of cathedral and parochial altars in the Church of England had no cross or crucifix on them during the seventeenth and eighteenth centuries and the early part of the nineteenth century, although there is considerable evidence for the use of a pair of candlesticks during that period.[5] There are also many instances of altar pieces which were furnished with a painting, but rarely, if ever, is the Crucifixion depicted in post-Reformation Anglican practice.[6] (See Plate 34.)

In eighteenth-century French liturgical writings we encounter complaints about the crowding of altars with crosses and six candlesticks, which were still considered a novelty.[7] Thus Anglican tradition and French liturgical practice of that period still display a conservative restraint in keeping down to a minimum the ornaments on the altar.

---

[1] Mansi: IX, 793, *Ut Corpus Domini in altaris non in imaginario ordine sed sub crucis titulo componantur*, See also, D. Rock: *The Church of our Fathers*, Vol. I, p. 92.

[2] Cf. W. S. Porter: *The Gallican Rite* (1958), p. 41.

[3] *Hierurgia Anglicana*, ed. V. Staley (1902), pt. I, pp. 65-9.   [4] Ibid., p. 73.

[5] D. R. Dendy, *The Use of Lights in Christian Worship* (1959), pp. 151-175. See also G. W. O. Addleshaw: *The High Church Tradition*, p. 53.

[6] G. W. O. Addleshaw and F. Etchells: *The Architectural Setting of Anglican Worship*, p. 159.

[7] L. A. Bocquillot: *Traité Historique de La Liturgie Sacrée* (Paris, 1701), pp. 103-5.

In so doing there was a following of the most venerable traditions of Christendom that nothing should stand on the altar save what was required for the celebration of the mysteries.

It was not until the second phase of the Oxford Movement in the middle of the last century that it began to be assumed that there was something 'correct' in having a cross standing on, or immediately over all altars. Had the facts that we have set out in this chapter been more widely recognized much litigation and controversy would have been avoided. Nowadays it is not unknown for an altar to be furnished with a standing cross, while behind or over the altar there is a sculptured reredos with a crucifix in the midst, and over the reredos there is a stained glass window with the Crucifixion depicted therein. This multiplication of the symbol of our redemption tends to cheapen its essential purpose. It is also timely to recall that the chief function of the Christian altar is to offer the Eucharistic sacrifice, and not simply to be a mere pediment to support vast crosses and candlesticks in silver or silver-gilt.

A special kind of processional cross is that carried before Archbishops and Metropolitans. Its use has been traced back to the time of St. Gregory the Great (d. 604), and it is possible that there are references to its use in the lives of St. Caesarius of Arles and St. Samson of Dol.

In a number of medieval effigies and pictures of deceased Archbishops the Primate is shown holding his cross. But this has been done to show that he is a Primate and not simply a bishop. In normal practice the Archbishop has his Primatial Cross borne before him by his chaplain, while he himself carries his crozier. In giving the blessing the Primate holds his crozier, and his chaplain continues to carry the cross. There is no ancient authority restricting the use of the crozier to the diocese of which the bishop is diocesan, since it is a symbol of a bishop's office and not one of mere jurisdiction.

SELECT BIBLIOGRAPHY

M. Andrieu: *Les Ordines Romani du Haut Moyen Age*, 5 vols. (Louvain, 1931–61).

E. Bishop: *Liturgica Historica* (1918), article, The Christian Altar.

J. Braun: *Der christliche Altar in seiner geistlichen Entwicklung* (Munich, 1924).

L. Bréhier: *Les Origines du Crucifix dans l'art religieux* (Paris, 1904).

L. Bréhier: *L'Art Chrétien* (Paris, 1928), 2nd ed.

F. Cabrol and H. Leclercq: *Dictionnaire d'Archéologie Chrétienne et de Liturgie*, 15 vols. (Paris, 1907–53), quoted as D.A.C.L.

R. Garruci: *Storia dell' arte cristiana*, 6 vols. (Prato, 1872–82).

M. Gough: *The Early Christians* (London, 1961).

H. O'Neill Hencken: *The Archaeology of Cornwall and Scilly* (1932).

F. Henry: *La Sculpture Irlandaise pendant les douze premiers siècles de l' Ère Chrétienne*, 2 vols. (Paris, 1932).

J. E. Hunt: *English and Welsh Crucifixes*, 670–1550 (1956).

E. Mâle: *L'Art Religieux du XIIIe siècle* (Paris, 1913); *L'Art Religieux du XIIe siècle* (Paris, 1922).

J. D. Mansi: *Sacrorum Conciliorum nova et amplissima Collectio*, 31 vols., Florence, 1759–1798, quoted as Mansi.

J. P. Migne: *Patrologia Latina* (Paris, 1844 et seqq.), quoted as P.L.

J. P. Migne: *Patrologia Graeca* (Paris, 1844 et seqq.), quoted as P.G.

A. K. Porter: *Spanish Romanesque Sculpture*, 2 vols. (Florence, 1928).

V. E. Nash-Williams: *The Early Christian Monuments of Wales* (Cardiff, 1950).